THE *Fantastic* CUTAWAY BOOK OF SPACECRAFT

Nigel Hawkes and Alex Pang

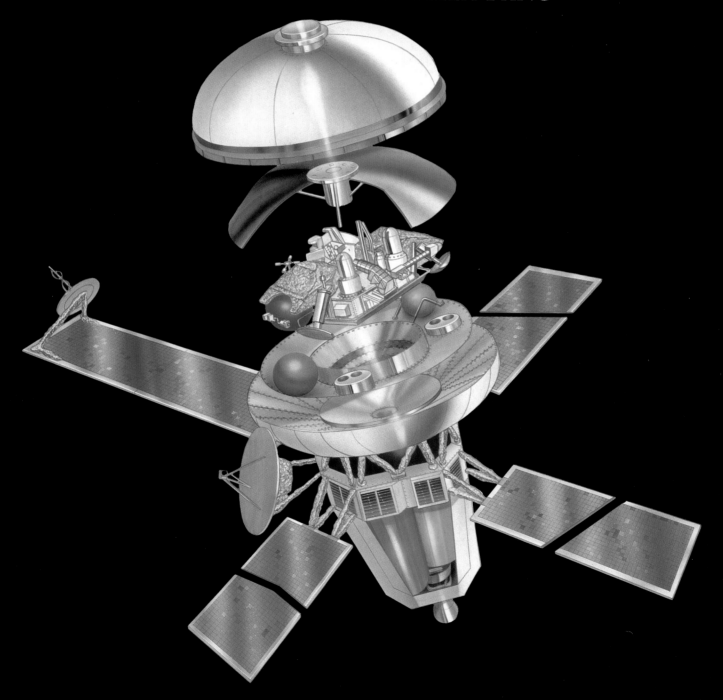

COPPER BEECH BOOKS
BROOKFIELD, CONNECTICUT

First published in the United States in 1995 by Copper Beech Books, an imprint of The Millbrook Press, 2 Old New Milford Road, Brookfield, Connecticut 06804

Editor Jon Richards
Design David West Children's Book Design
Designer Ed Simkins
Picture research Brooks Krikler Research
Illustrators Alex Pang and Ian Thompson

Library of Congress Cataloging-in-Publication Data
Hawkes, Nigel. 1943-
The fantastic cutaway book of spacecraft / by Nigel Hawkes : illustrated by Alex Pang.
p. cm. Includes index.
Summary: Cutaway illustrations and text reveal how the space shuttle and other spacecraft work and what astronauts do in space.
ISBN 1-56294-903-9. --
ISBN 1-56294-935-7 (pbk.)
1. Space vehicles--Juvenile literature. [1. Space vehicles. 2. Astronautics.] I. Pang, Alex, ill. II. Title.
TL793.H368   1995   95-24052
629.47--dc20   CIP AC

CONTENTS

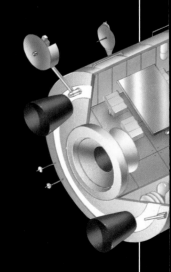

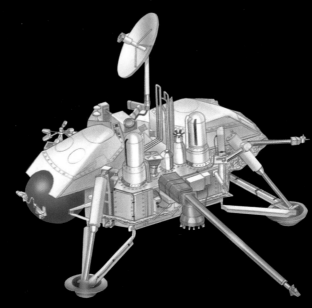

INTRODUCTION

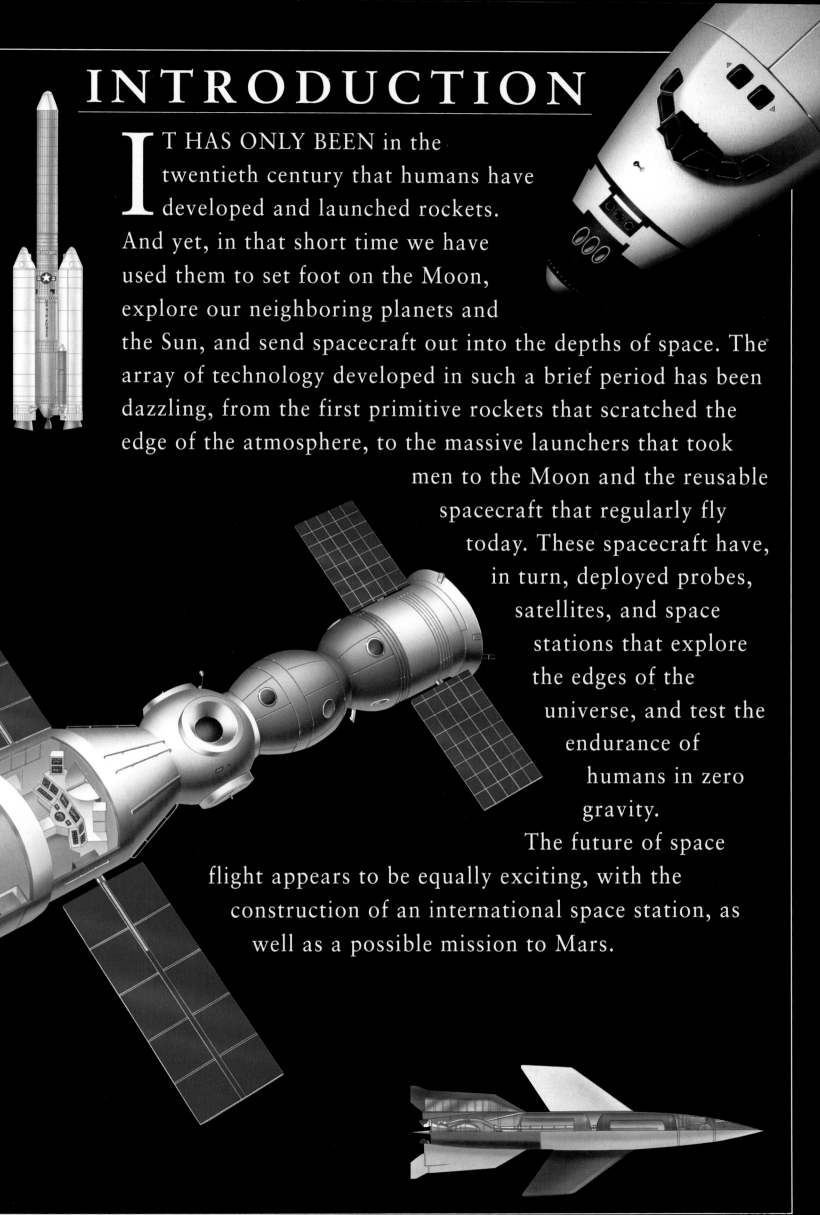

IT HAS ONLY BEEN in the twentieth century that humans have developed and launched rockets. And yet, in that short time we have used them to set foot on the Moon, explore our neighboring planets and the Sun, and send spacecraft out into the depths of space. The array of technology developed in such a brief period has been dazzling, from the first primitive rockets that scratched the edge of the atmosphere, to the massive launchers that took men to the Moon and the reusable spacecraft that regularly fly today. These spacecraft have, in turn, deployed probes, satellites, and space stations that explore the edges of the universe, and test the endurance of humans in zero gravity.

The future of space flight appears to be equally exciting, with the construction of an international space station, as well as a possible mission to Mars.

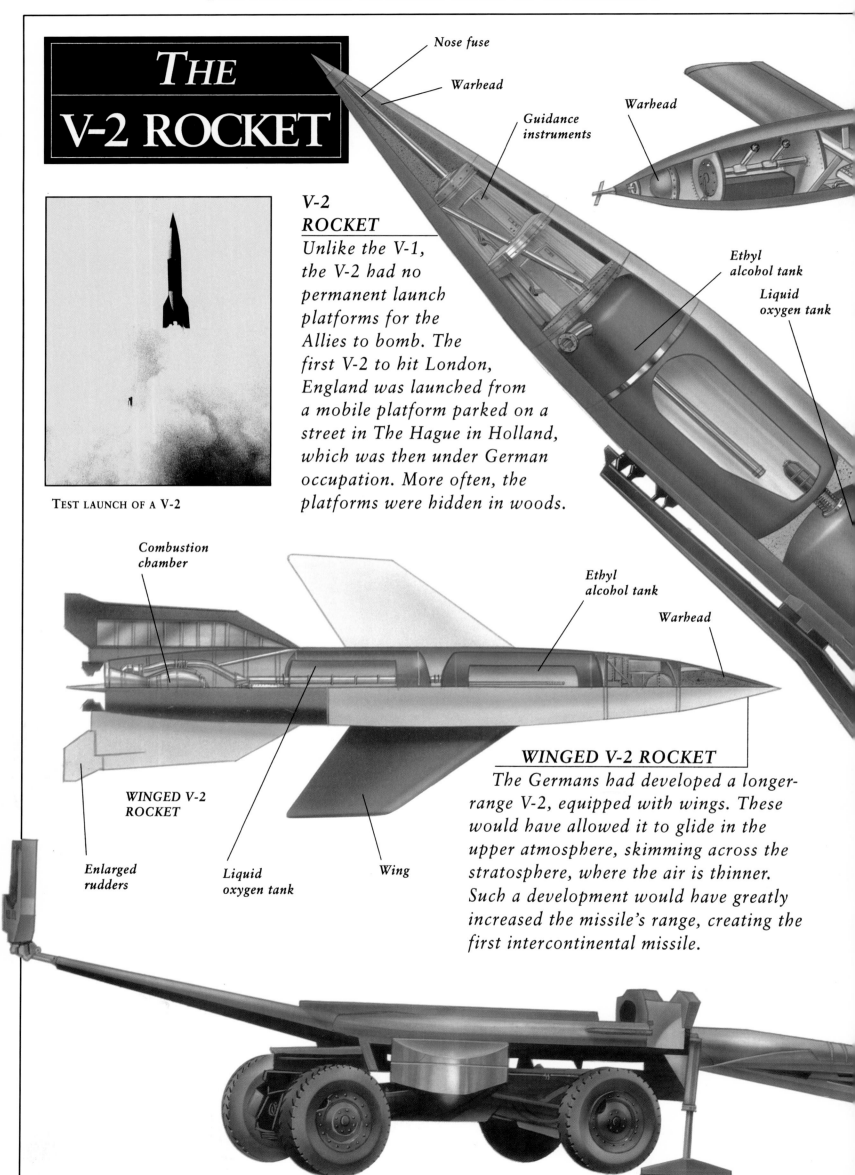

THE V-2 ROCKET

Nose fuse

Warhead

Guidance instruments

Warhead

Ethyl alcohol tank

Liquid oxygen tank

TEST LAUNCH OF A V-2

V-2 ROCKET

Unlike the V-1, the V-2 had no permanent launch platforms for the Allies to bomb. The first V-2 to hit London, England was launched from a mobile platform parked on a street in The Hague in Holland, which was then under German occupation. More often, the platforms were hidden in woods.

Combustion chamber

Ethyl alcohol tank

Warhead

WINGED V-2 ROCKET

Enlarged rudders

Liquid oxygen tank

Wing

WINGED V-2 ROCKET

The Germans had developed a longer-range V-2, equipped with wings. These would have allowed it to glide in the upper atmosphere, skimming across the stratosphere, where the air is thinner. Such a development would have greatly increased the missile's range, creating the first intercontinental missile.

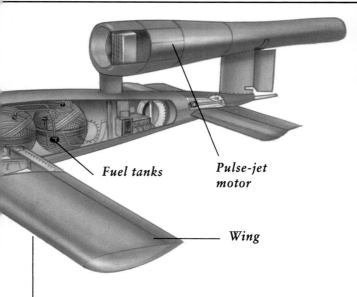

Fuel tanks

Pulse-jet motor

Wing

V-1 FLYING BOMB

The "doodlebug" was a flying bomb which was easy to make, and did not require a pilot. Launched from ramps, the V-1s had pulse-jet, not rocket, engines which were designed to stop once they reached their target. Unlike V-2s, they flew slowly enough to be shot down. In the summer of 1944, nearly 190 were launched every day.

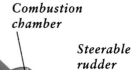

Combustion chamber

Steerable rudder

Mobile launcher

DEVASTATION AFTER A V-2 ATTACK ON LONDON

ARRIVING WITHOUT WARNING at 3,500 mph (5,600 kmh), the V-2 rocket was one of the most terrifying weapons of World War II (1939–1945). The V-2 was launched vertically from a mobile platform, and reached a height of 60 miles (96 km) and a range of about 200 miles (320 km). By following a high, arched path, the missile traveled about 200 miles (320 km). It delivered a 2,200 pound (998 kg) warhead that was capable of causing tremendous damage. Between September 1944 and March 1945, more than 4,300 were launched against Antwerp, Paris, and London (above). The technology behind the V-2 proved the start of space exploration, and was used by both the United States and the Soviet Union after the war. The rocket's designer, Wernher von Braun, was taken to the United States, where he played an important role in the American space program.

EARLY HISTORY OF ROCKETS

V-2 TEST AT PEENEMÜNDE

PEENEMÜNDE
The greatest leaps in rocket technology were made by the Germans during World War II. They designed and tested their rockets at Peenemünde, in Germany, near the Baltic Sea coast.

THE FIRST ROCKETS *that burned gunpowder, were developed by the Chinese as early as A.D. 1000. The modern rocket was the work of three men: Konstantin E. Tsiolkovsky (Russian), Johannes Winkler (German), and Robert H. Goddard (American). Tsiolkovsky realized that to leave the atmosphere would require a multi-stage rocket, one that was able to jettison most of its mass, and leave only a small, final stage to go into orbit. Winkler and Goddard developed the liquid-fuel rockets. In these fuel and an oxidizer are mixed and* burned. This creates exhaust, which escapes through a nozzle to produce thrust. Goddard built the first liquid-fuel rocket in 1926.

GODDARD AND HIS 1926 ROCKET

KONSTANTIN E. TSIOLKOVSKY

GIRD-X ROCKET

RUSSIAN ROCKETS
Sergei Korolev was the engineer who helped the Soviet Union become a leader in rocketry. His first rockets were launched in the 1930s, and by 1956 he had built the SS-6, which was to launch the first satellite, Sputnik, on October 4, 1957.

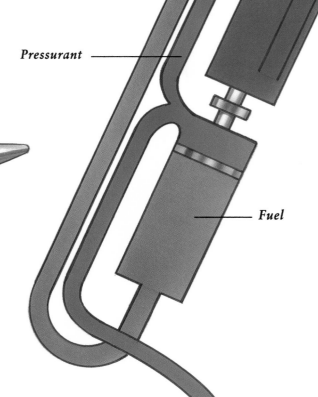
Exhaust gases

GODDARD'S 1926 ROCKET

Liquid oxygen

Pressurant

Fuel

Combustion chamber

Nozzle

U.S. SATELLITES

The United States was slower than the Soviet Union to get into space. Attempts to launch a Vanguard rocket in 1957 failed, and in desperation the U.S. Government turned to V-2 designer Wernher von Braun, now living in the United States. Three weeks after Sputnik 1, von Braun's group at the Army Ballistic Missile Agency in Huntsville, Alabama, was given permission to launch two satellites. The first, Explorer 1, reached orbit on January 31, 1958, just one day behind schedule. It was launched by a Jupiter-C rocket, a direct descendant of the V-2. Von Braun's rocket development reached a peak with the construction of the Saturn rockets that carried the Apollo missions to the Moon.

VANGUARD 1

SPUTNIK

To prove that humans could fly in space, the Soviets first launched a dog, Laika, in Sputnik 2, on November 3, 1957, even though they knew they had no chance of bringing the animal back to Earth alive. Laika died after ten days in space, when the oxygen ran out. But medical sensors sent back information showing that the dog had survived the high-gravity forces at lift-off, and the weightlessness of space. The launch paved the way for the first manned mission in 1961.

LAIKA

VANGUARD ROCKET

JUNO

Some of the earliest American satellites were launched using the Juno rocket, a modified Army Redstone ballistic missile. Compared to the Russian launch vehicles, the Juno rockets were small. This meant that the Explorer satellites they carried also had to be small, the first weighed a mere 31lbs (14kg). To achieve this, many instruments had to be miniaturized.

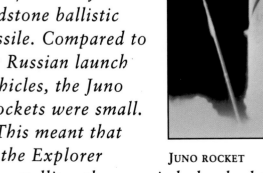

JUNO ROCKET

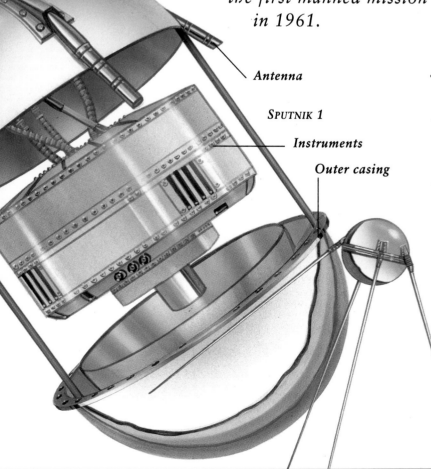

Antenna

SPUTNIK 1

Instruments

Outer casing

THE VOSTOK 1 CAPSULE

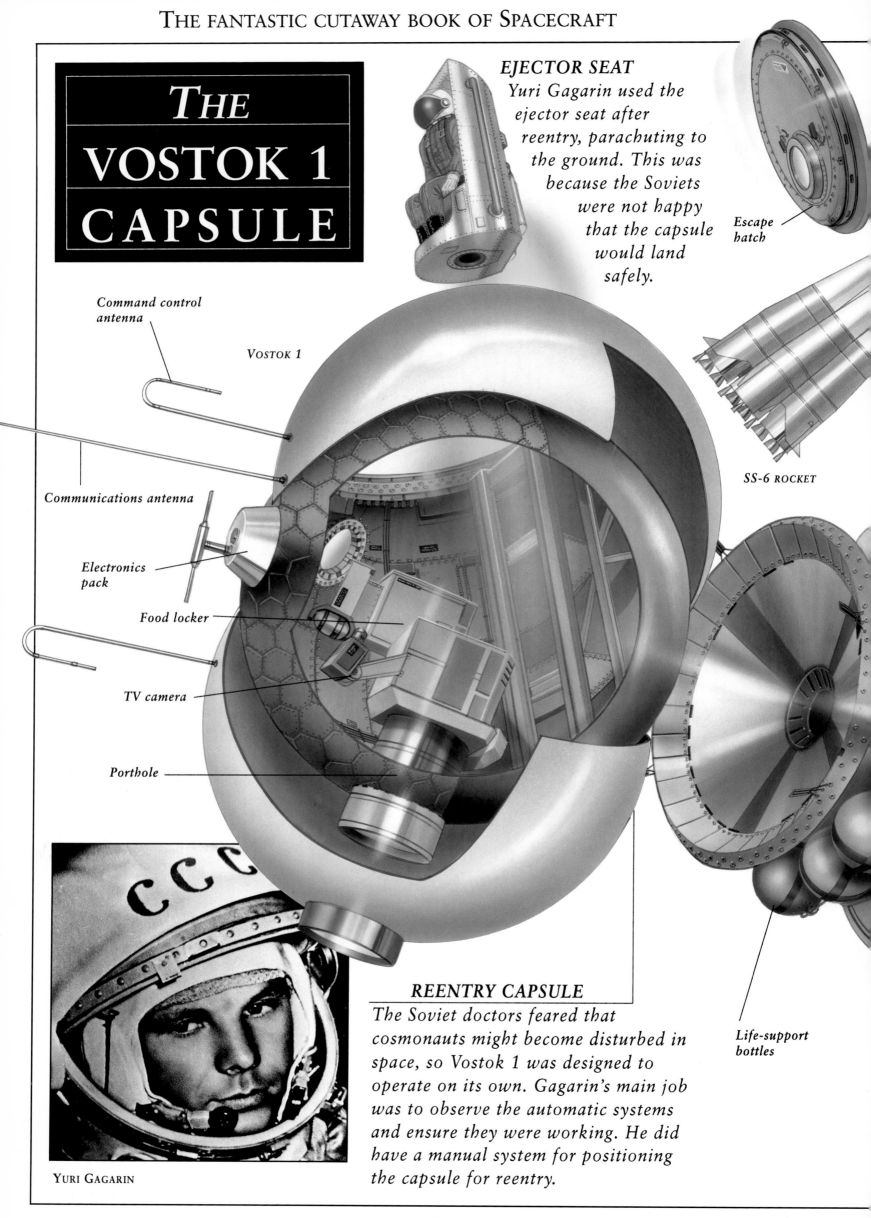

EJECTOR SEAT

Yuri Gagarin used the ejector seat after reentry, parachuting to the ground. This was because the Soviets were not happy that the capsule would land safely.

Escape hatch

VOSTOK 1

Command control antenna

Communications antenna

Electronics pack

Food locker

TV camera

Porthole

SS-6 ROCKET

Life-support bottles

YURI GAGARIN

REENTRY CAPSULE

The Soviet doctors feared that cosmonauts might become disturbed in space, so Vostok 1 was designed to operate on its own. Gagarin's main job was to observe the automatic systems and ensure they were working. He did have a manual system for positioning the capsule for reentry.

Vostok capsule ————

LAUNCHER

Vostok was launched by an A-1 launcher – an SS-6 missile fueled by liquid oxygen and kerosene with an extra stage on top. The rocket suffered several failures before Gagarin's historic flight on April 12, 1961.

EQUIPMENT MODULE

The equipment module held everything not required in the reentry module. This included the nitrogen and oxygen life-support bottles, batteries for the radios and instruments. It also held the retro-rockets that slowed the spacecraft and took it out of orbit.

LAUNCH OF VOSTOK 1

THE REENTRY CAPSULE AFTER THE MISSION

VOSTOK ("EAST") was the capsule used by Yuri Gagarin for the first manned space orbit. It was launched by an SS-6 missile, with a third stage on top. The SS-6 was designed by Korolev as an intercontinental ballistic missile that was 20 times as powerful as the V-2. Its core, 9 ft (2 m) in diameter and 80 ft (24 m) long, was surrounded by four strap-on boosters. Vostok I was a spherical capsule with an equipment module attached. To come safely out of orbit, Vostok used retro-rockets to slow down and a heat shield to resist the searing heat of reentering the atmosphere (above).

EQUIPMENT MODULE

Retro-rocket

THIRD STAGE

THE RACE TO THE MOON

LUNA 3

Luna 3 was powered by solar cells rather than batteries and was accurately guided into orbit around the Moon. On October 10, 1959, it transmitted the first pictures of the dark side of the Moon (below).

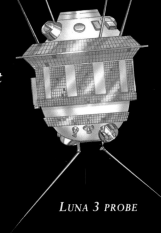

LUNA 3 PROBE

T HE MOON, our nearest neighbor in space, has always been an object of fascination and mystery. In his book, From the Earth to the Moon, *Jules Verne* wrote about a group fired to the Moon by an artillery shell (above) – which in real life would have killed them. In the late 1950s, the struggle to reach the Moon first started the Space Race between the U.S. and the Soviet Union.

JULES VERNE'S MOON TRIP

A-2 LUNIK ROCKET

FAR SIDE OF THE MOON

LUNA PROBES

Luna 3's picture was taken by an ordinary camera, developed on board, then scanned and beamed back to Earth. Though of poor technical quality, it showed a huge crater, later named after Tsiolkovsky. The first soft landing on the Moon was made by Luna 9 in 1966, after many failures. TV cameras on board took pictures of the lunar surface, showing a rough and pitted landscape. However, there was no evidence of the deep dust that scientists feared might have prevented manned landings in the future. Subsequent Luna missions explored much of the Moon, and even returned with lunar samples.

LUNA 1 AND LUNA 2

The first vehicle to get close to the Moon was Luna 1. Designed to crash into the Moon for propagandistic purposes, it carried no scientific instruments. But it missed by 4,000 miles (6,400 km). Luna 2, launched the same year, succeeded.

LUNA 2 PROBE

MERCURY AND GEMINI

The first American astronauts were launched in the Mercury capsules, proving U.S. ability to put men in space and bring them back alive. Led by John Glenn, the Mercury astronauts made several missions, the longest lasting over 34 hours. The original Mercury capsules were replaced by Gemini which, as the name implies, carried two astronauts. These missions tested skills, such as docking, that were to prove vital in the preparation for a lunar mission. In 1968, the huge Saturn V rocket, with only two unmanned tests behind it, took three Apollo 8 astronauts to the Moon. They went into lunar orbit before returning home. Now all was ready for the Moon landing, which the United States had promised to achieve before the end of the decade.

MERCURY ATLAS ROCKET

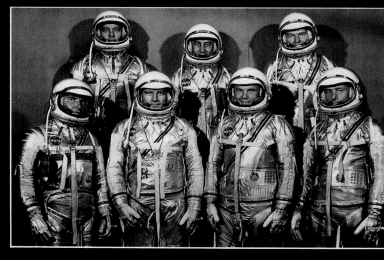

THE MERCURY ASTRONAUTS

FIRST ASTRONAUTS

The original Mercury astronauts were Scott Carpenter, Leroy Cooper, John Glenn, Virgil Grissom, Walter Schirra, Alan Shepard, and Donald Slayton. Shepard flew in Apollo 14, Slayton was part of the Apollo-Soyuz Test Project, and Grissom died in the Apollo 1 fire at Cape Canaveral.

LUNA 16

Luna 16 was a Soviet unmanned probe that landed on the Moon on September 20, 1970, took samples, and brought them back. It was a triumph, but by then the United States had landed men on the Moon.

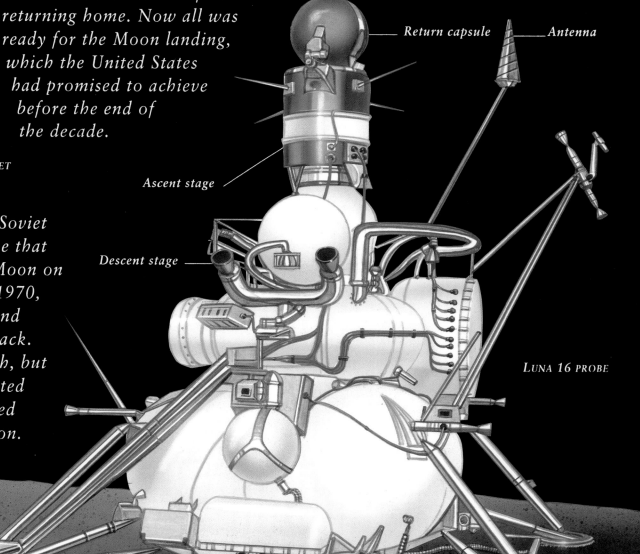

Return capsule — Antenna

Ascent stage

Descent stage

LUNA 16 PROBE

Drilling device

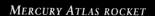

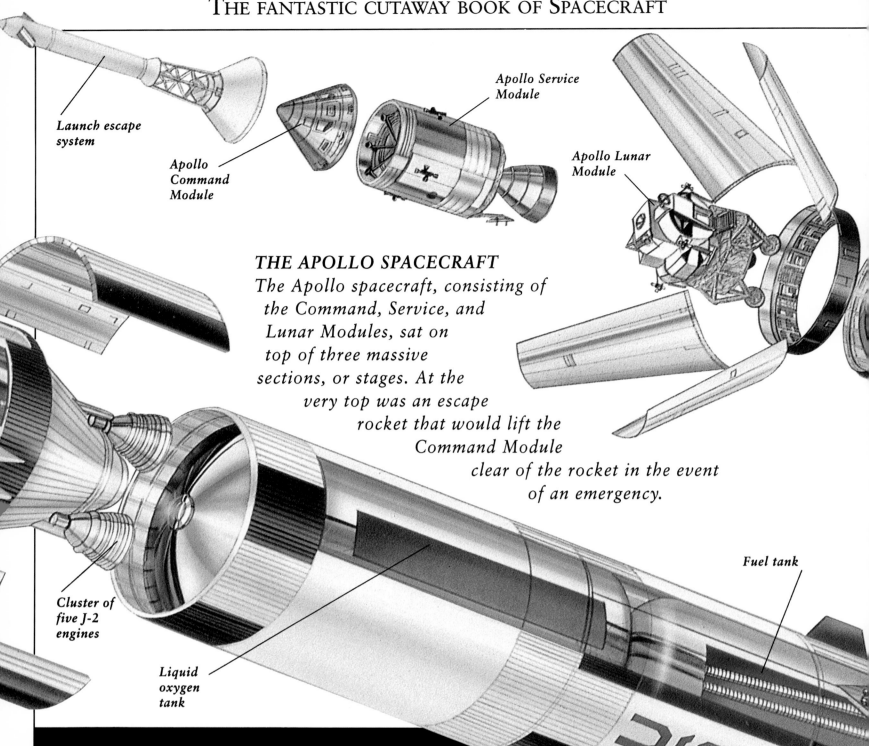

Launch escape
system

Apollo
Command
Module

Apollo Service
Module

Apollo Lunar
Module

THE APOLLO SPACECRAFT
*The Apollo spacecraft, consisting of
the Command, Service, and
Lunar Modules, sat on
top of three massive
sections, or stages. At the
very top was an escape
rocket that would lift the
Command Module
clear of the rocket in the event
of an emergency.*

Fuel tank

Cluster of
five J-2
engines

Liquid
oxygen
tank

THE MIGHTY SATURN V, which
first put men on the Moon, flew just thirteen
times between 1968 and 1973. It stood 363 ft
(110 m) tall, carried more than 2,000 tons of
fuel, and could lift more than 140 tons into
Earth orbit. The first stage had five F-1 engines,
burning 15 tons of fuel per second, lifting it
clear of the launchpad (right). At a height of
39 miles (62.5 km) the second-stage rockets
ignited, carrying the spacecraft to a height of
115 miles (184 km), then the third-stage engines
took it into low earth orbit. A final burn of the
rockets took the astronauts in the Apollo craft
on their way to the Moon.

LIFT-OFF OF APOLLO 11

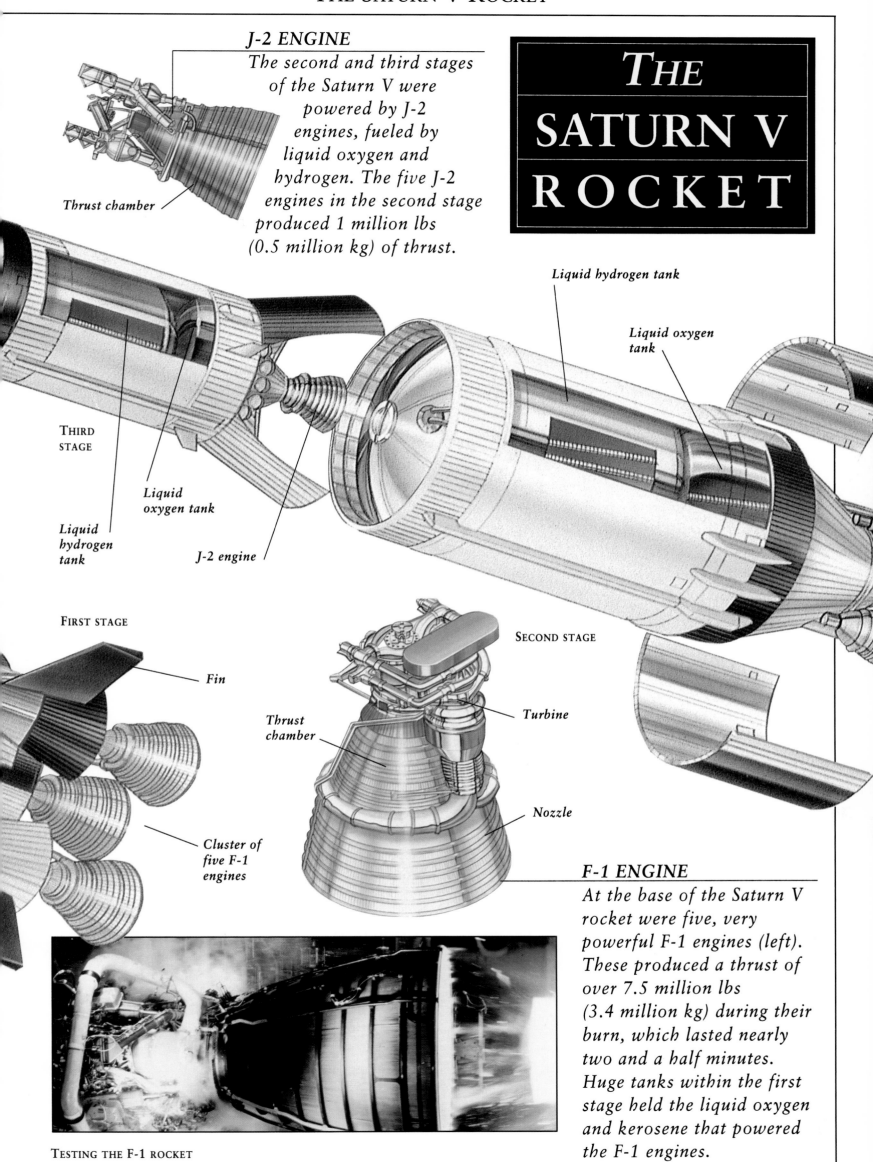

J-2 ENGINE

The second and third stages of the Saturn V were powered by J-2 engines, fueled by liquid oxygen and hydrogen. The five J-2 engines in the second stage produced 1 million lbs (0.5 million kg) of thrust.

Thrust chamber

THE SATURN V ROCKET

Liquid hydrogen tank

Liquid oxygen tank

THIRD STAGE

Liquid oxygen tank

Liquid hydrogen tank

J-2 engine

FIRST STAGE

SECOND STAGE

Fin

Turbine

Thrust chamber

Nozzle

Cluster of five F-1 engines

F-1 ENGINE

At the base of the Saturn V rocket were five, very powerful F-1 engines (left). These produced a thrust of over 7.5 million lbs (3.4 million kg) during their burn, which lasted nearly two and a half minutes. Huge tanks within the first stage held the liquid oxygen and kerosene that powered the F-1 engines.

TESTING THE F-1 ROCKET

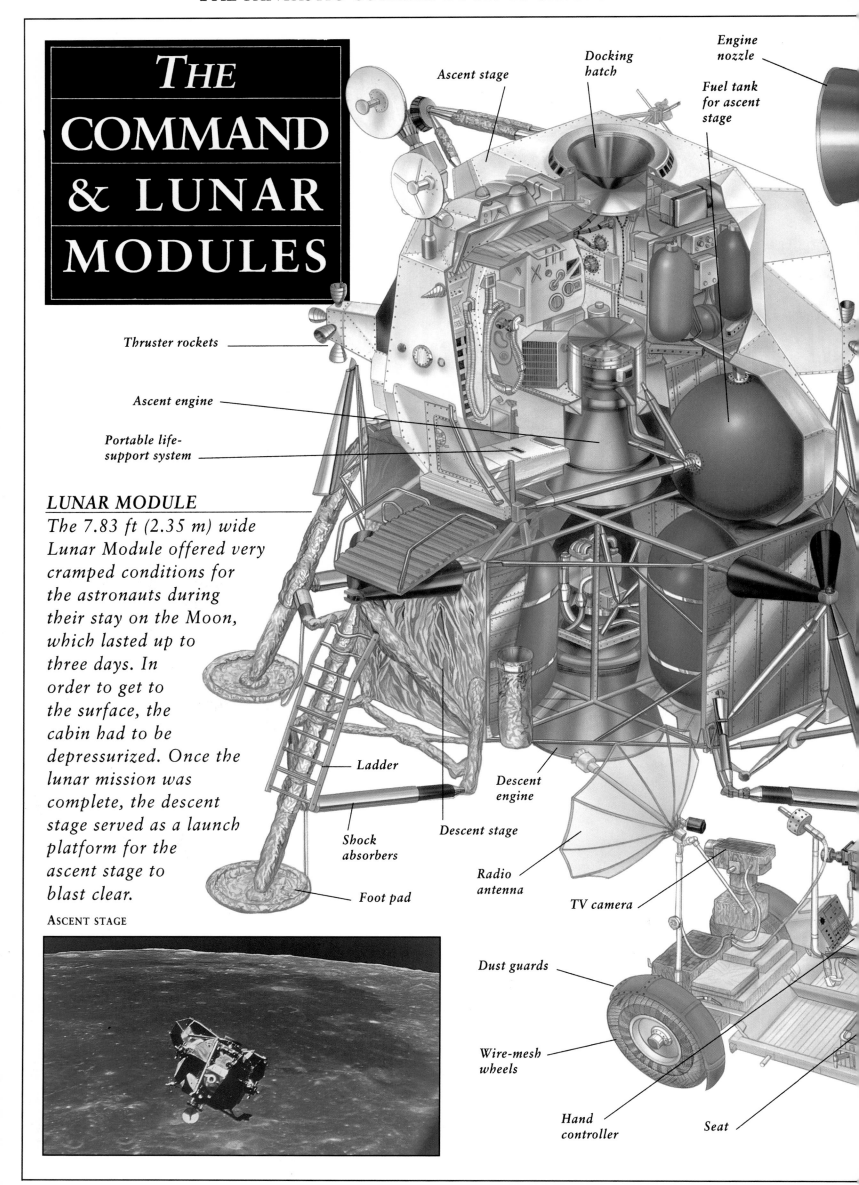

THE COMMAND & LUNAR MODULES

Ascent stage

Docking hatch

Engine nozzle

Fuel tank for ascent stage

Thruster rockets

Ascent engine

Portable life-support system

LUNAR MODULE

The 7.83 ft (2.35 m) wide Lunar Module offered very cramped conditions for the astronauts during their stay on the Moon, which lasted up to three days. In order to get to the surface, the cabin had to be depressurized. Once the lunar mission was complete, the descent stage served as a launch platform for the ascent stage to blast clear.

ASCENT STAGE

Ladder

Shock absorbers

Foot pad

Descent engine

Descent stage

Radio antenna

TV camera

Dust guards

Wire-mesh wheels

Hand controller

Seat

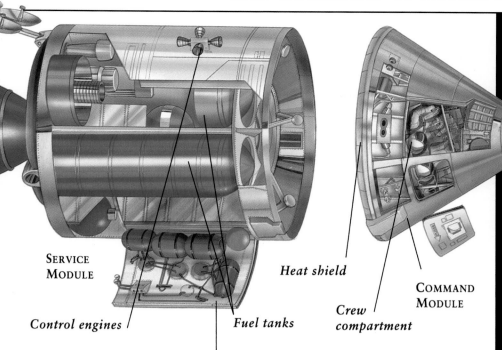

SERVICE MODULE

Control engines

Fuel tanks

Heat shield

Crew compartment

COMMAND MODULE

COMMAND AND SERVICE MODULES

The Command Module held the three astronauts on their way to the Moon. Beneath this was the Service Module that held the fuel and life-support systems for the mission (right). This was discarded before reentry into the Earth's atmosphere.

COMMAND AND SERVICE MODULES

LUNAR ROVER EXPLORES THE MOON'S SURFACE

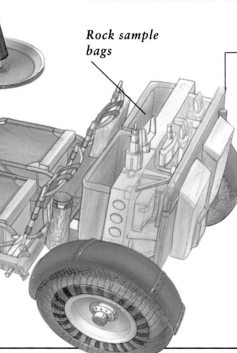

Rock sample bags

LUNAR ROVER

On the last three Apollo missions the astronauts took a vehicle which looked like a simple dune buggy (above). This allowed them to travel further across the Moon's surface to explore and collect rock samples. It had a top speed of about 9 mph (14 km/h) and was stored within the descent stage of the Lunar Module.

THE ASTRONAUTS traveled to the Moon in a spacecraft made up of three parts: the Command, Service, and Lunar Modules. Only the Lunar Module actually landed on the Moon, while the Command and Service Modules remained linked together in orbit. Three astronauts flew, but only two landed. Once the lunar mission was complete, they took off again in the ascent stage of the Lunar Module, leaving the remainder on the Moon. They linked up with the Command Module in lunar orbit for the homeward journey back to Earth. The Service Module was detached and left in Earth's orbit, while the final descent to splashdown in the Pacific Ocean was made in the Command Module (below).

SPLASHDOWN IN THE PACIFIC OCEAN

THE LAUNCH VEHICLES

Launchers have steadily grown in size, from the A-1 that launched Vostok to the huge Energia, flown only twice before the decline of the Soviet Union. Today powerful launchers, such as Delta, are needed to put communications satellites (each weighs five tons) into a geostationary orbit 23,000 miles (36,800 km) above the Earth. Produced in Europe, the Ariane series are the most successful commercial launchers and have launched more than 100 satellites. With the decreasing cost of rocket technology, space has now grown into an important industry, with many countries and companies using a huge variety of launchers, competing for trade.

DELTA ROCKET

Fairing

Third stage

SATELLITE LAUNCH

Solid-fuel boosters produce most of the takeoff thrust, burn out quickly, and then separate. The rocket reaches orbit with the help of the upper-stage engines, which fire as the spent stages fall away. Finally, the fairings, which have protected the satellite, open to release it into orbit.

Second stage

Solid-fuel boosters

First stage

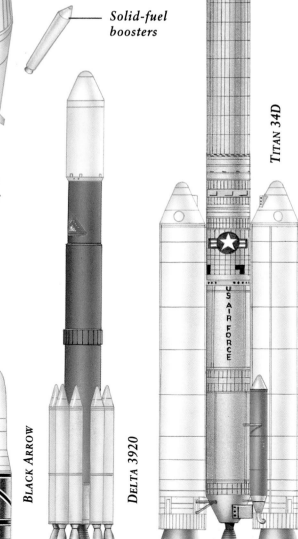

Feet
30
20
10
0

A-1 SPUTNIK

JUNO 1

CSL-1 LONG MARCH

BLACK ARROW

DELTA 3920

TITAN 34D

Deployed
satellite

MISSION CONTROL AT KOUROU, FRENCH GUIANA

SPACE CENTERS

Launch sites near the Equator are best, because the Earth's rotation speed is faster here. This means a rocket launched from the Equator requires less thrust to reach orbit than one launched further north or south. Ariane launches, from Kourou, in French Guiana, can lift a cargo weighing 10 percent more than from the Kennedy Space Center in Florida, because it is closer to the Equator.

LAUNCHERS

The United States and the former Soviet Union are not the only nations to have built their own launch systems. China, Japan, and India have all developed launchers. The Chinese CZ-4 lifts about four tons into low Earth orbit. The Indian ASLV failed on its first launch in 1986 and was abandoned. Japan has developed several launchers; the most powerful able to put a two-ton satellite into a geostationary orbit. England launched one small satellite in 1971, on its Black Arrow launcher.

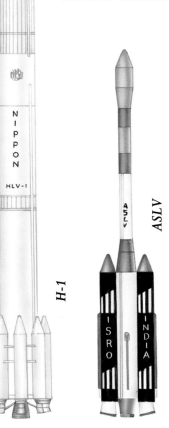

H-1

ASLV

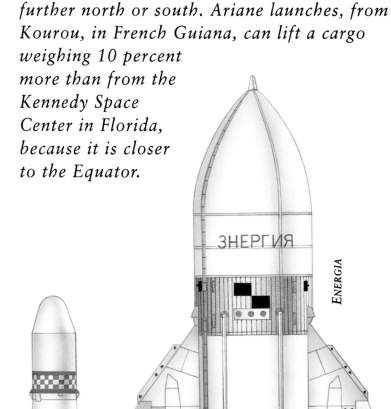

ARIANE-4

CZ-4

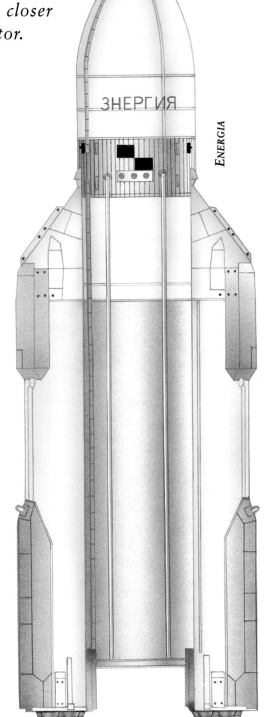

ENERGIA

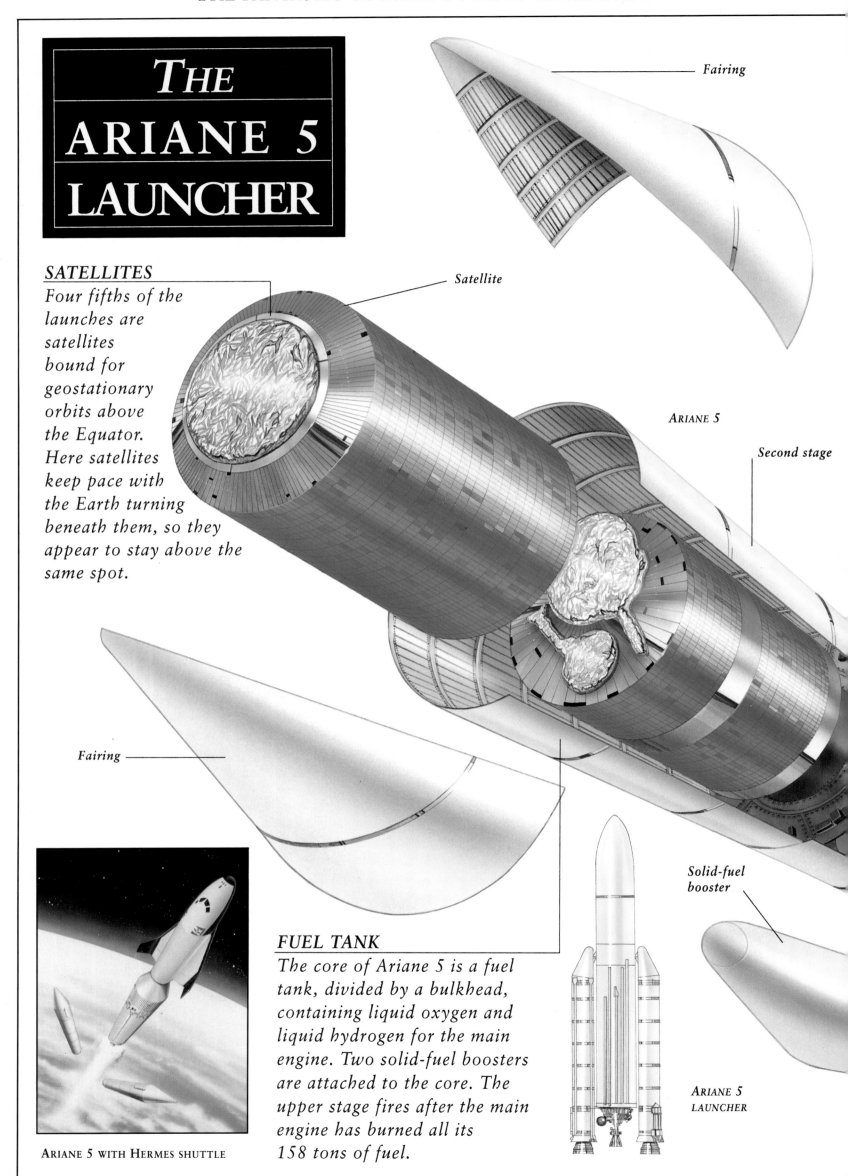

THE ARIANE 5 LAUNCHER

Fairing

SATELLITES

Four fifths of the launches are satellites bound for geostationary orbits above the Equator. Here satellites keep pace with the Earth turning beneath them, so they appear to stay above the same spot.

Satellite

ARIANE 5

Second stage

Fairing

Solid-fuel booster

FUEL TANK

The core of Ariane 5 is a fuel tank, divided by a bulkhead, containing liquid oxygen and liquid hydrogen for the main engine. Two solid-fuel boosters are attached to the core. The upper stage fires after the main engine has burned all its 158 tons of fuel.

ARIANE 5 WITH HERMES SHUTTLE

ARIANE 5 LAUNCHER

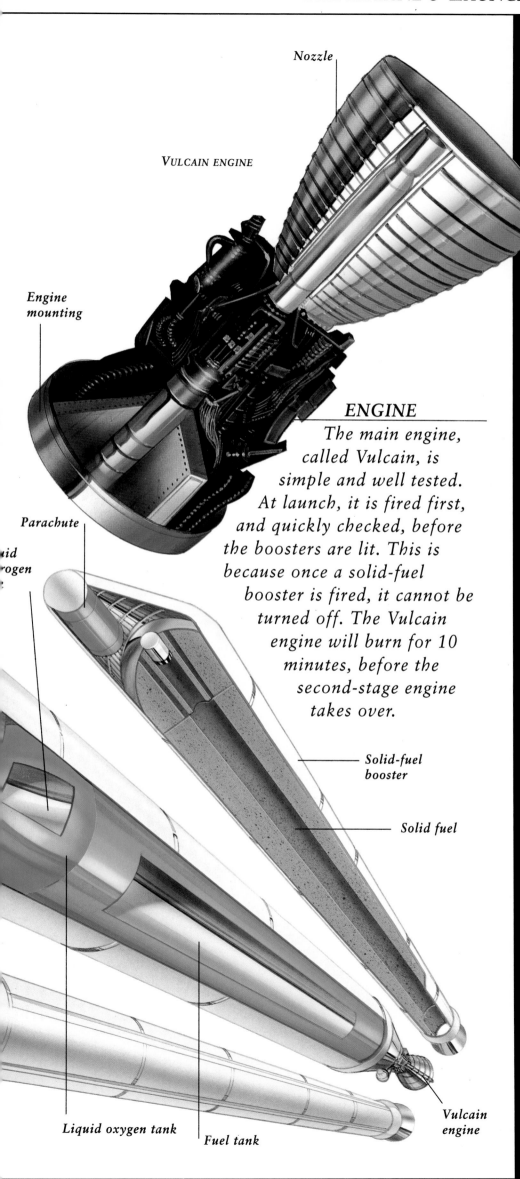

Nozzle

VULCAIN ENGINE

Engine
mounting

Parachute

...id
...ogen
...

ENGINE
The main engine, called Vulcain, is simple and well tested. At launch, it is fired first, and quickly checked, before the boosters are lit. This is because once a solid-fuel booster is fired, it cannot be turned off. The Vulcain engine will burn for 10 minutes, before the second-stage engine takes over.

Solid-fuel
booster

Solid fuel

Liquid oxygen tank

Fuel tank

Vulcain
engine

A MULTI-PURPOSE, two-stage launcher, Ariane 5 will be able to put two satellites at once – a total of 6 tons – into a geostationary orbit. Alternatively it could launch a 20-ton satellite or a manned vehicle, such as the Hermes craft (bottom left) into low orbit, or send unmanned scientific missions to the planets. After launch from the site at Kourou (below), the combination of solid-fuel boosters and the main engines take Ariane 5 to an altitude of 43 miles (70 km) before the boosters separate and are recovered. Then at 88 miles (140 km) the upper-stage ignites, boosting the craft into a higher orbit.

KOUROU LAUNCH SITE, FRENCH GUIANA

REUSABLE SPACECRAFT

X-1

ROCKETS that are used only once are an expensive way to get into space. A space plane that could take off from an airport, reach space, and then fly home again would be more economical. In theory, the space shuttle should be cheaper. But the cost of servicing it means that some conventional launchers are a cheaper alternative.

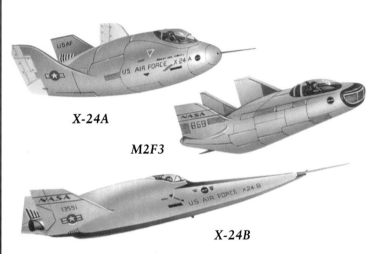

X-24A

M2F3

X-24B

THE X-PLANES
Starting in 1946, the United States developed a series of high-performance rocket planes capable of reaching the edge of space (some of the pilots were given astronaut's wings!). The X-planes were carried by adapted bombers, such as the B-29 or B-52, released at high altitude, and then flown under rocket power to great heights and enormous speeds. The Bell X-1 (top), piloted by Chuck Yeager, was the first aircraft to break the speed of sound, on October 14, 1947. The last of the series, the X-15 (right) reached a height of 67 miles (109 km) and a speed of 4,520 mph (7,232 km/h). Other X-planes included the X-24A, M2F3, and X-24B (above).

THE SOVIET SPACE PLANE
The Soviet Union designed and built a small-scale, unmanned shuttle which had its first flight in 1982. Sometimes called the Kosmolyet, this one-ton spacecraft was designed to test the heat shields and reentry techniques for the full-size shuttle Buran, then under development. Kosmolyet was only about 10 ft (3 m) long, with an 8 ft (2.5 m) wingspan.

KOSMOLYET AND SL8 BOOSTER

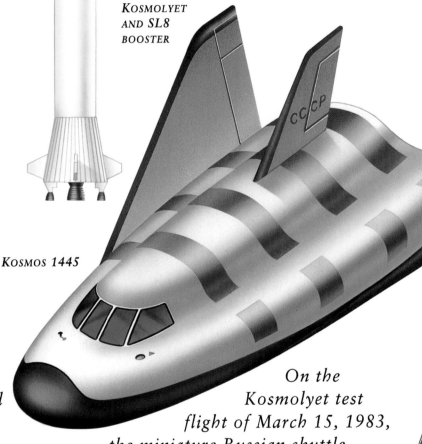

KOSMOS 1445

On the Kosmolyet test flight of March 15, 1983, the miniature Russian shuttle splashed down in the Indian Ocean and was picked up by Soviet ships. Australian planes took pictures of the mysterious spacecraft.

X-15 AND CONVERTED B52

SOVIET SHUTTLE

The Soviet shuttle Buran (the Russian word for "Snowstorm") looked uncannily similar to the U.S. shuttle when it made its only flight in November 1988. Launched by the Energia booster from Baikonur (right), it made two

BURAN AND ENERGIA

unmanned orbits under automatic control, before landing. All parts of the Energia launcher were recovered, including the fuel tank, which returned to Earth by parachute. Buran itself, which has no rocket motors, glided to a landing after a flight of three hours and 25 minutes at a specially-built runway 8 miles (13 km) from the launchpad (below).

SPACE PLANES

Subsequent designs for reusable spacecraft include the design of space planes. These would climb to a high altitude using conventional jet engines. Then, when the atmosphere was

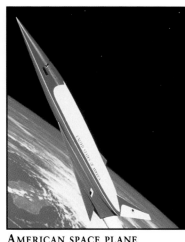

AMERICAN SPACE PLANE

too thin for jet engines to work, rocket motors would take over, taking the plane into a low orbit. Once outside the atmosphere, the plane could reach incredible speeds, traveling to the other side of the world in a couple of hours.

ESA HERMES

BURAN FLIGHT PROFILE

HERMES

One proposed project is the development of the French-designed space plane called Hermes. It would be 65 ft (20 m) long, carry a crew of two or three and a payload of about five tons, and dock with the international space station Alpha. Hermes will play a vital role in carrying replacement crews and supplies to the space station, once it has been built. However, financial problems have meant delays for the development of the project.

21

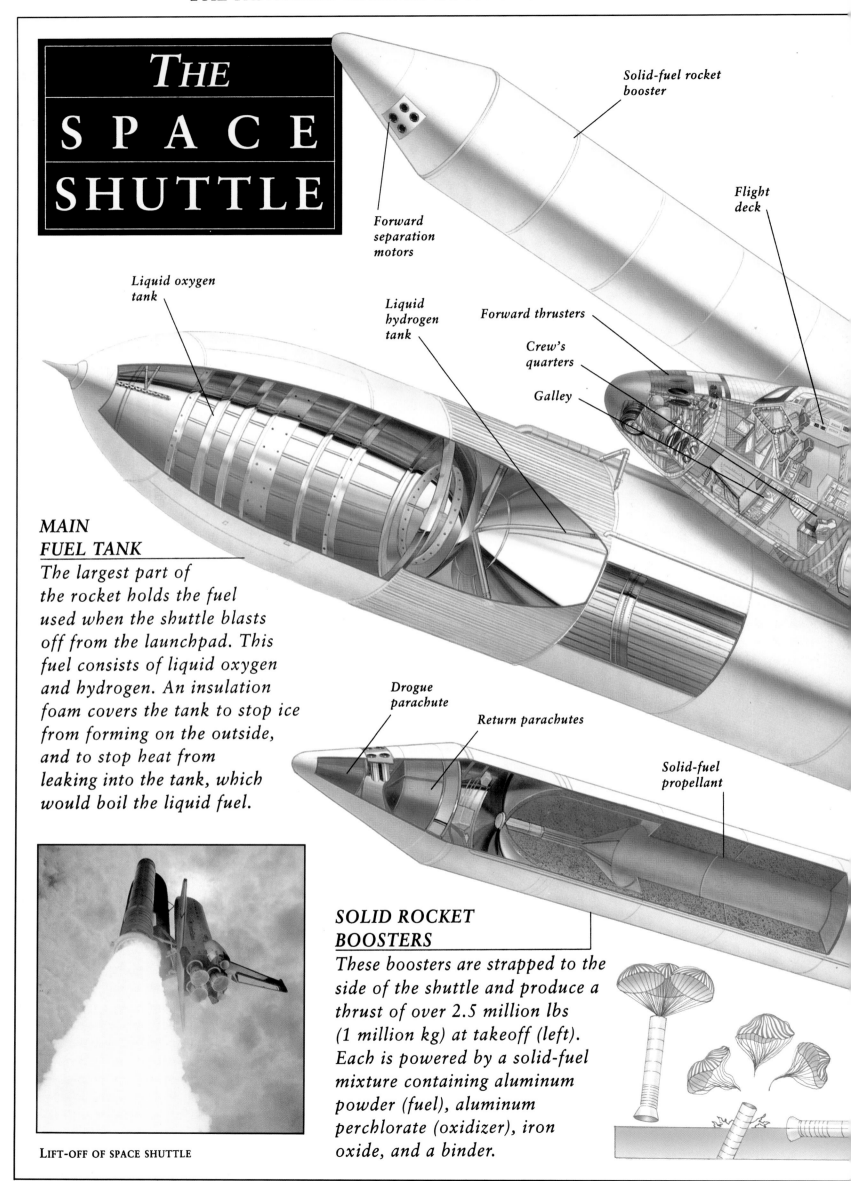

THE SPACE SHUTTLE

Solid-fuel rocket booster

Flight deck

Forward separation motors

Liquid oxygen tank

Liquid hydrogen tank

Forward thrusters

Crew's quarters

Galley

MAIN FUEL TANK

The largest part of the rocket holds the fuel used when the shuttle blasts off from the launchpad. This fuel consists of liquid oxygen and hydrogen. An insulation foam covers the tank to stop ice from forming on the outside, and to stop heat from leaking into the tank, which would boil the liquid fuel.

Drogue parachute

Return parachutes

Solid-fuel propellant

SOLID ROCKET BOOSTERS

These boosters are strapped to the side of the shuttle and produce a thrust of over 2.5 million lbs (1 million kg) at takeoff (left). Each is powered by a solid-fuel mixture containing aluminum powder (fuel), aluminum perchlorate (oxidizer), iron oxide, and a binder.

LIFT-OFF OF SPACE SHUTTLE

THE SHUTTLE

The shuttle can put a cargo and a crew of up to seven people (right) into an orbit between 115 and 690 miles (185 and 1,110 km) above the planet. Its cargo bay can hold satellites or even a space laboratory.

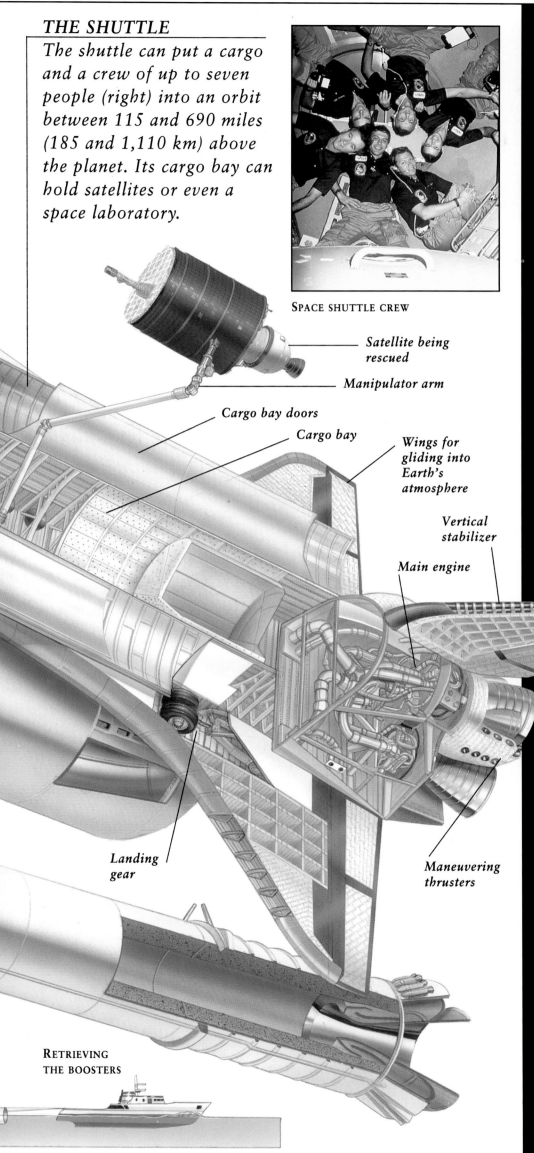

SPACE SHUTTLE CREW

Satellite being rescued

Manipulator arm

Cargo bay doors

Cargo bay

Wings for gliding into Earth's atmosphere

Vertical stabilizer

Main engine

Landing gear

Maneuvering thrusters

RETRIEVING THE BOOSTERS

THE SPACE SHUTTLE is a combination of a launcher, a plane, and a manned spacecraft. At launch, it is attached to a huge fuel tank and two solid-fuel boosters. Once in orbit it can maneuver, carry out tasks, then reenter the atmosphere and glide to land on a 3 mile (5 km) runway (bottom). Weighing over 68 tons, the shuttle is the heaviest, and the most expensive glider ever built. The idea behind the shuttle was to make space flight simpler and cheaper.

However, even though everything except the main fuel tank can be reused, each shuttle craft costs $1.1 billion, and it still costs $250 million to launch a satellite using the space shuttle, no less than a conventional rocket.

SPACE SHUTTLE LANDING

THE SHUTTLE MISSION

The shuttle has shown itself versatile in a number of roles, including docking space station Mir, in June 1995. All has not been successful, however. The 25th shuttle flight, in January 1986, ended in disaster when the shuttle Challenger blew up just after launch, killing all seven astronauts on board. The accident required a re-design of many of the spacecraft's systems, and delayed any further shuttle flights until September 1988. The shuttle will now play a major role in the building of the new space station, Alpha. It will carry the station's modules, as well as deliver supplies and astronauts.

Shuttle enters Earth's orbit

Fuel tank is jettisoned

MISSION PROFILE

At launch, all five of the shuttle's engines fire. The two boosters, each 150 ft (45 m) long, are jettisoned at an altitude of 28 miles (45 km). The three main engines continue firing, producing a combined thrust of 470,000 lbs (213,152 kg). Once all the liquid fuel is used up, the main tank is jettisoned at a height of 68 miles (109 km). Then the shuttle's maneuvering rockets and 44 tiny thrusters are used to put it into its final orbit. Once in orbit, the mission can last between 7 and 30 days. During this time, satellite launches, experiments, or rescues occur in and around the cargo bay, which is 15 ft (4.5 m) wide and 60 ft (18 m) long. A robot arm, controlled from the rear of the flight deck, enables satellites to be lifted from the cargo bay and released into orbit. It can also retrieve a satellite should it require repairing, as in the case of the Hubble Space Telescope, which was fixed in December 1993.

Boosters jettisoned

Lift-off from launch pad

LIFT-OFF OF SPACE SHUTTLE

SHUTTLE CARRIED "PIGGYBACK" BY A JUMBO JET

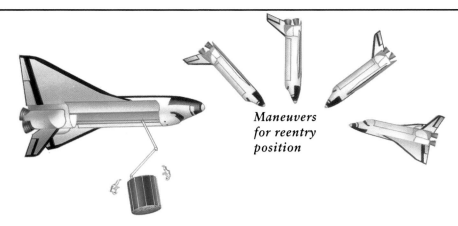

Maneuvers for reentry position

LAUNCHING SATELLITES

The shuttle can only launch satellites into a low Earth orbit. Should a satellite need to reach an orbit beyond the shuttle's range, then the satellite can be fitted with solid-fuel rockets, which fire when it is a safe distance from the shuttle.

RETURN TO EARTH

To land, the shuttle uses its maneuvering system to slow down. It is fired with the shuttle going backward, so it must be turned around to face the right way. This is done with the reaction control system – three sets of twelve tiny thrusters, one set at the front and two at the rear. During reentry, outside temperatures can rise to 2,732°F (1,500°C), and the shuttle is protected by some 32,000 tiles. The shuttle then glides to Earth, landing at more than 200 mph (320 km/h).

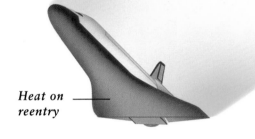

Heat on reentry

LAUNCHING A SATELLITE

SPACE LABS

The European Spacelab (below), which can be carried by the shuttle, contains a pressurized laboratory that is 9 ft (2.7 m) long. It is used to carry out experiments that harness the zero gravity found in orbit. These include the production of pure medicines and making stellar observations.

Shuttle glides to Earth

Shuttle lands

After landing in California, the shuttle is taken back to Cape Canaveral, in Florida, on the back of a specially converted Boeing 747 Jumbo jet. Here the shuttle is extensively refitted before being attached to a new fuel tank and boosters that have been retrieved.

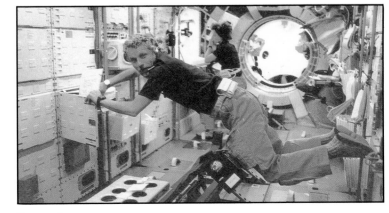

INSIDE SPACELAB

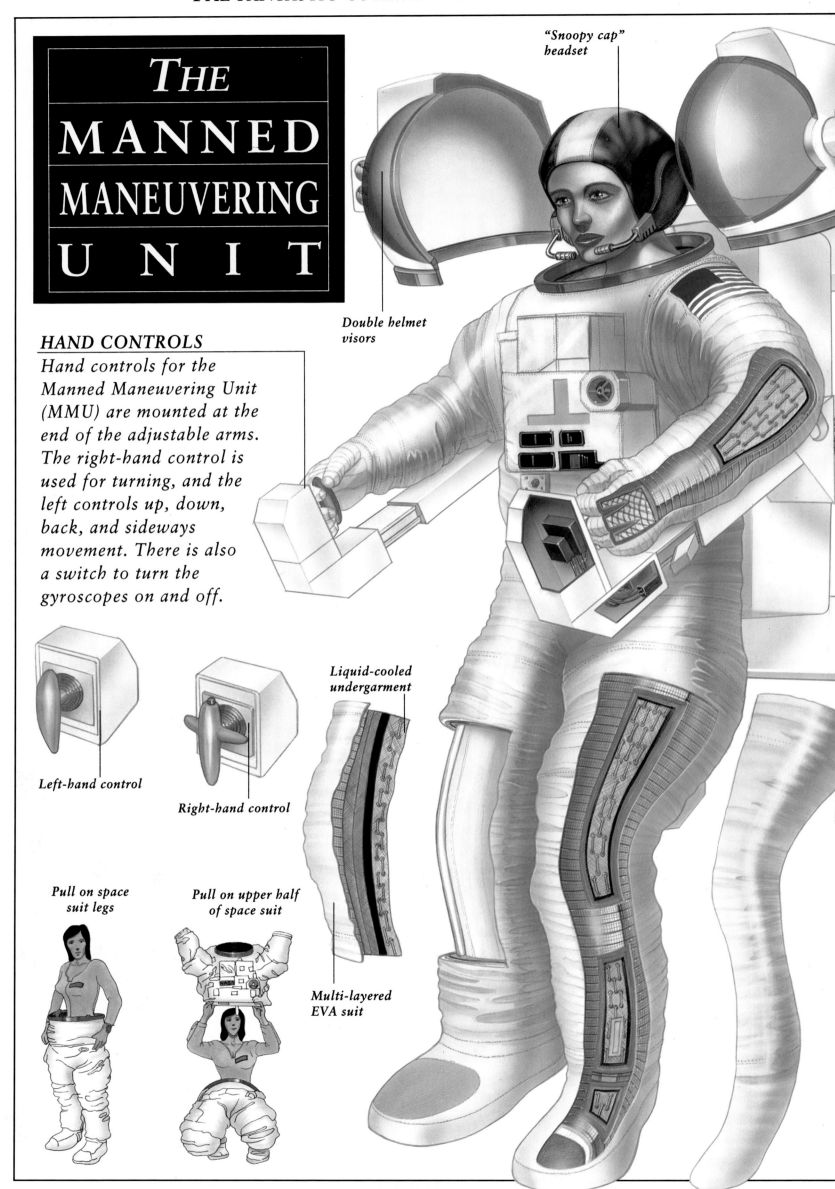

"Snoopy cap" headset

Double helmet visors

THE MANNED MANEUVERING UNIT

HAND CONTROLS

Hand controls for the Manned Maneuvering Unit (MMU) are mounted at the end of the adjustable arms. The right-hand control is used for turning, and the left controls up, down, back, and sideways movement. There is also a switch to turn the gyroscopes on and off.

Left-hand control

Right-hand control

Liquid-cooled undergarment

Multi-layered EVA suit

Pull on space suit legs

Pull on upper half of space suit

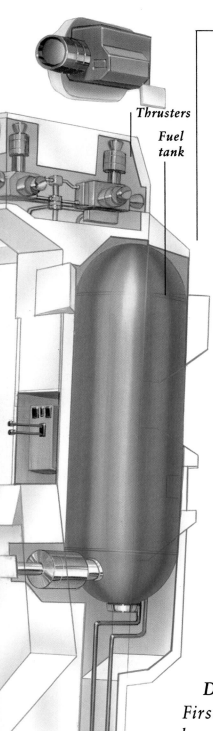

Thrusters

Fuel tank

THE MMU

Nitrogen gas is fired through 24 small nozzles to propel the MMU outside the space shuttle. The MMU has sufficient gas for flying around the shuttle several times, or for two round-trips between the shuttle and another object. The nitrogen can be refilled in the cargo bay.

THE MANNED MANEUVERING UNIT

PUTTING ON AN EVA SUIT

DRESSING

First the astronaut puts on a one-piece undergarment, which includes a urine-collection receptacle. Next come the legs and then he or she slides into the torso and backpack section. Finally, the "Snoopy cap" and helmet are put on.

TO MOVE ABOUT in space, astronauts need pressurized space suits, and for some missions they have also used the Manned Maneuvering Unit (MMU). This is like an armchair that locks onto the back of the space suit, equipped with jet thrusters that allow the astronaut to move or turn. The MMU is also equipped with power outlets and attachment points for lights, cameras, and tools. The MMU was first used on February 7, 1984, when astronaut Bruce McCandless became the first human satellite, flying up to 320 ft (98 m) away from the shuttle Challenger. Since then it has been used to recover satellites and "carry" them to the shuttle's cargo bay.

Put on helmet

Connect two halves

Put on "Snoopy cap" headset

Put on gloves

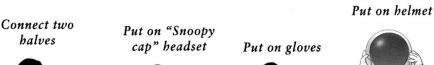

ABOVE THE EARTH'S ATMOSPHERE, the Hubble Space Telescope (HST) has supplied astronomers with information from the edges of the universe. Named after the American astronomer Edwin Hubble, the HST is a reflecting telescope that can see further and more clearly than any telescope on Earth. It can see objects 14 billion light years away, whose light has taken so long to reach us that we are looking at them as they were when the universe was born. Launched in 1990, there was despair when it was discovered that the main mirror of the HST was faulty. A mission by the shuttle Endeavor corrected it.

REPAIRING THE HUBBLE SPACE TELESCOPE

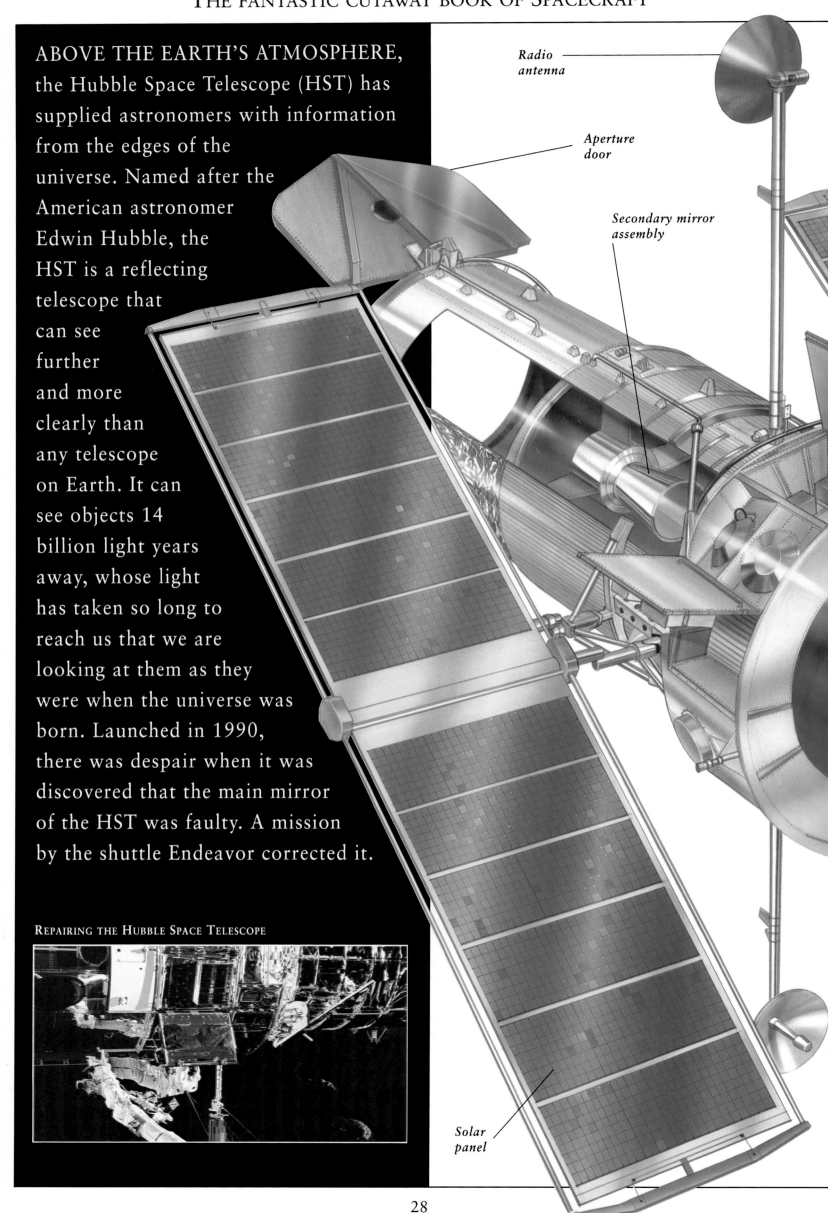

Radio antenna

Aperture door

Secondary mirror assembly

Solar panel

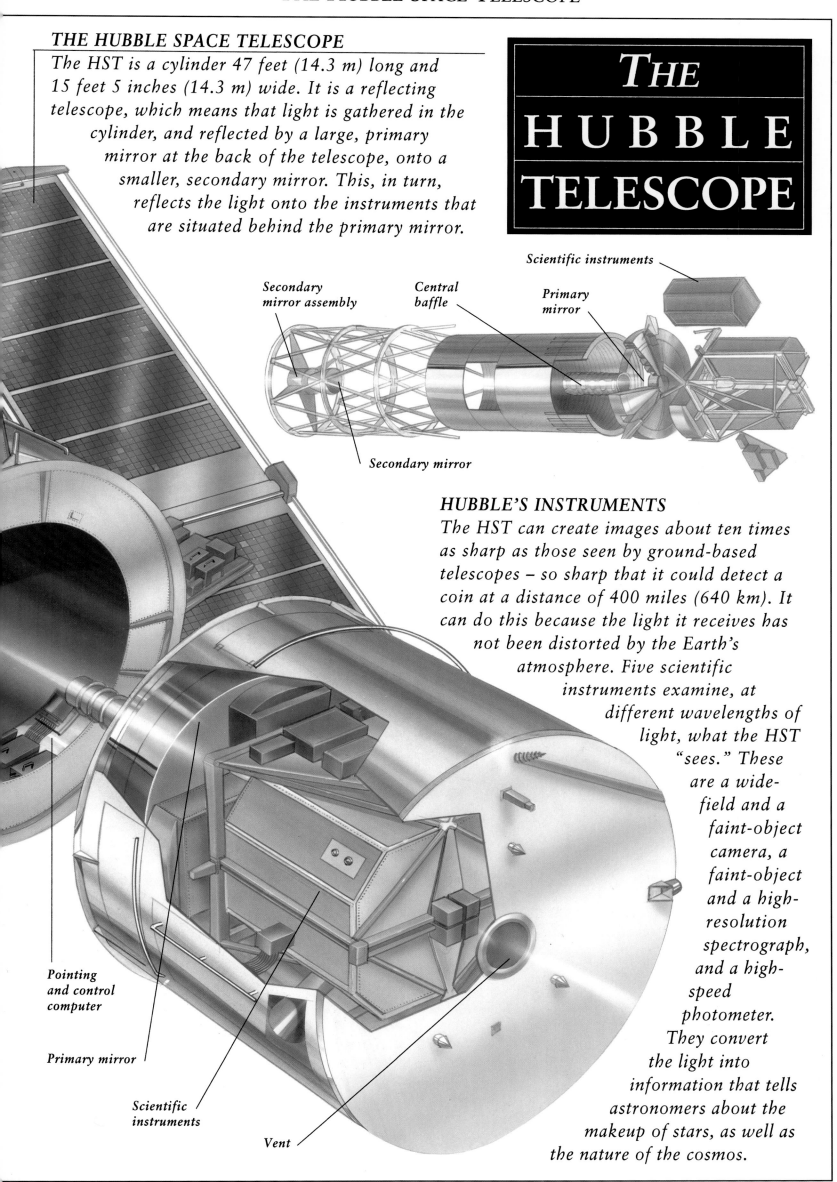

THE HUBBLE SPACE TELESCOPE

The HST is a cylinder 47 feet (14.3 m) long and 15 feet 5 inches (14.3 m) wide. It is a reflecting telescope, which means that light is gathered in the cylinder, and reflected by a large, primary mirror at the back of the telescope, onto a smaller, secondary mirror. This, in turn, reflects the light onto the instruments that are situated behind the primary mirror.

THE HUBBLE TELESCOPE

Scientific instruments

Secondary mirror assembly

Central baffle

Primary mirror

Secondary mirror

HUBBLE'S INSTRUMENTS

The HST can create images about ten times as sharp as those seen by ground-based telescopes – so sharp that it could detect a coin at a distance of 400 miles (640 km). It can do this because the light it receives has not been distorted by the Earth's atmosphere. Five scientific instruments examine, at different wavelengths of light, what the HST "sees." These are a wide-field and a faint-object camera, a faint-object and a high-resolution spectrograph, and a high-speed photometer. They convert the light into information that tells astronomers about the makeup of stars, as well as the nature of the cosmos.

Pointing and control computer

Primary mirror

Scientific instruments

Vent

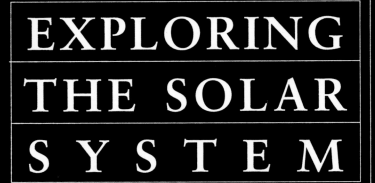

EXPLORING THE SOLAR SYSTEM

UNMANNED SATELLITES *have told us more about our solar system in the past forty years than we learned in the previous 400 years. What were once just tiny spots of light in the sky have been revealed as whole worlds, with their own atmospheres, climates, and moons. To date, all of the planets, except Pluto, have been visited and studied by spacecraft, as well as the sun, the asteroids, and even comets.*

TITAN LAUNCHER

VOYAGER

Two Voyager satellites, launched by Titan rockets (above), explored the giant planets – Jupiter, Saturn, Uranus, and Neptune. They saw volcanoes on Jupiter's moon, Io, and examined storms racing around Neptune. On Saturn they found new moons, and revealed the complexity of the planet's many rings.

GIOTTO

In 1986, the European satellite Giotto was one of a fleet of probes which studied Halley's comet. It flew within 335 miles (540 km) of the comet nucleus and took pictures, showing it to be a chunk of ice and dust, shaped like a peanut, some 9 miles (14 km) long and 5 miles (8 km) across.

HALLEY'S COMET

GIOTTO

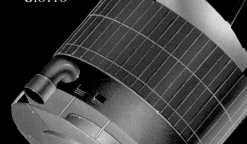

SATURN

PLUTO

NEPTUNE

URANUS

VOYAGER

THE SURFACE OF VENUS

VENERA

Venus is bright and easily seen from Earth, but it is enveloped in clouds and its surface cannot be studied. The Venera probes 7, 9, 10, 11, 12, 13, and 14 made soft landings and found that Venus had a rocky landscape, and an atmospheric pressure 90 times greater than that found on Earth.

SUN

MERCURY

VENERA

VENUS

EARTH

MARS

— PIONEER

JUPITER

PIONEER

Pioneers 10 and 11 were launched in 1972 and 1973 to study the outer reaches of the solar system. After completing their mission, they kept on going, leaving the solar system forever and continuing into interstellar space. Astonishingly, their signals continued to be picked up well into the 1990s. Both Pioneers carry a plaque (right) that shows a man and a woman, a hydrogen atom, a map of the solar system, and the position of the Sun relative to 14 stars.

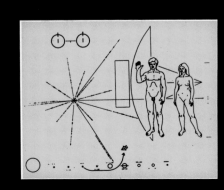

PIONEER PLAQUE

MAGELLAN AND GALILEO

Magellan went into orbit around Venus in 1990, and using radar to pierce the clouds, mapped the rugged surface of the planet. It revealed that most of Venus is covered by a cratered, low-lying plain. There are also two highland regions, Terra Ishtar and Terra Aphrodite, each about the size of Australia. Galileo,

LAUNCHING MAGELLAN

bound for Jupiter, took a remarkable picture of an asteroid, Gaspra, as it passed through the asteroid belt. The photograph showed it to be an irregular chunk of rock 12 miles (19 km) long by 7.5 miles (12 km) across. When it reached Jupiter in 1995, Galileo released a probe that pierced the planet's thick atmosphere, sending back information about the swarming clouds.

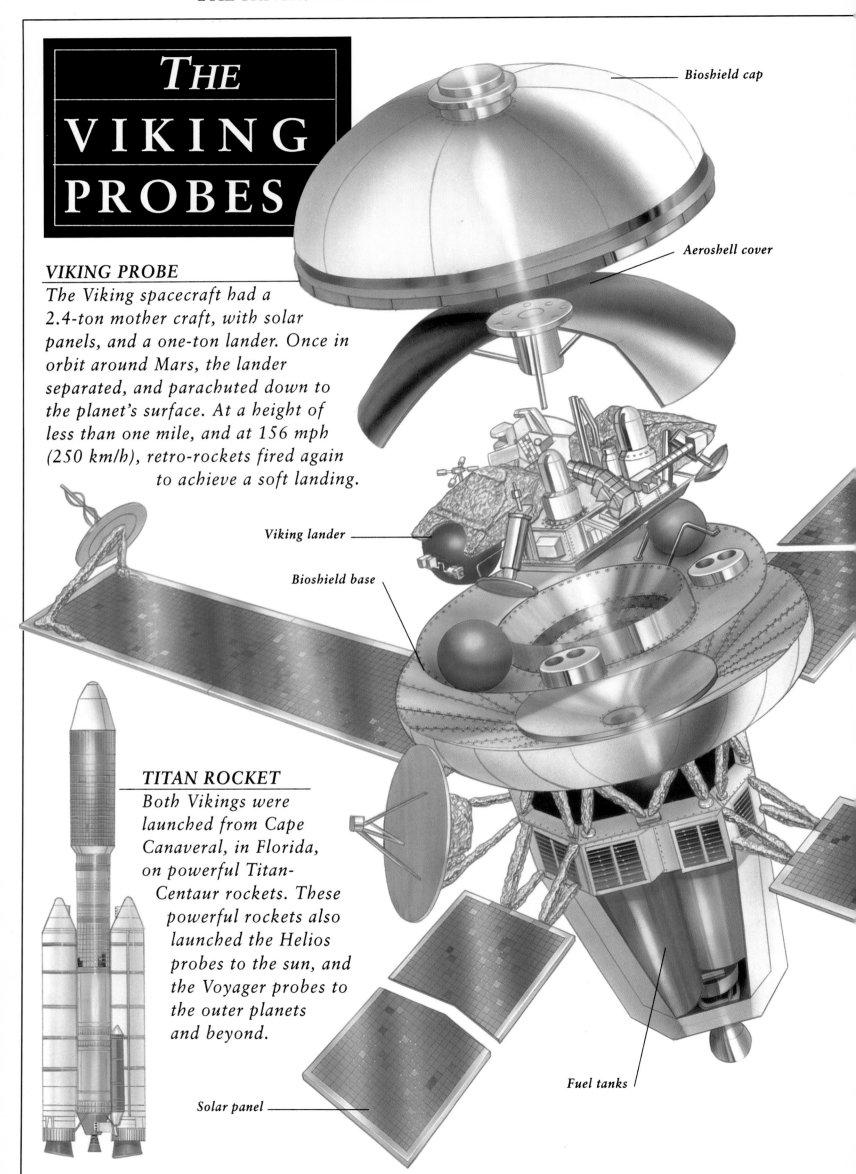

THE VIKING PROBES

VIKING PROBE

The Viking spacecraft had a 2.4-ton mother craft, with solar panels, and a one-ton lander. Once in orbit around Mars, the lander separated, and parachuted down to the planet's surface. At a height of less than one mile, and at 156 mph (250 km/h), retro-rockets fired again to achieve a soft landing.

TITAN ROCKET

Both Vikings were launched from Cape Canaveral, in Florida, on powerful Titan-Centaur rockets. These powerful rockets also launched the Helios probes to the sun, and the Voyager probes to the outer planets and beyond.

Bioshield cap

Aeroshell cover

Viking lander

Bioshield base

Fuel tanks

Solar panel

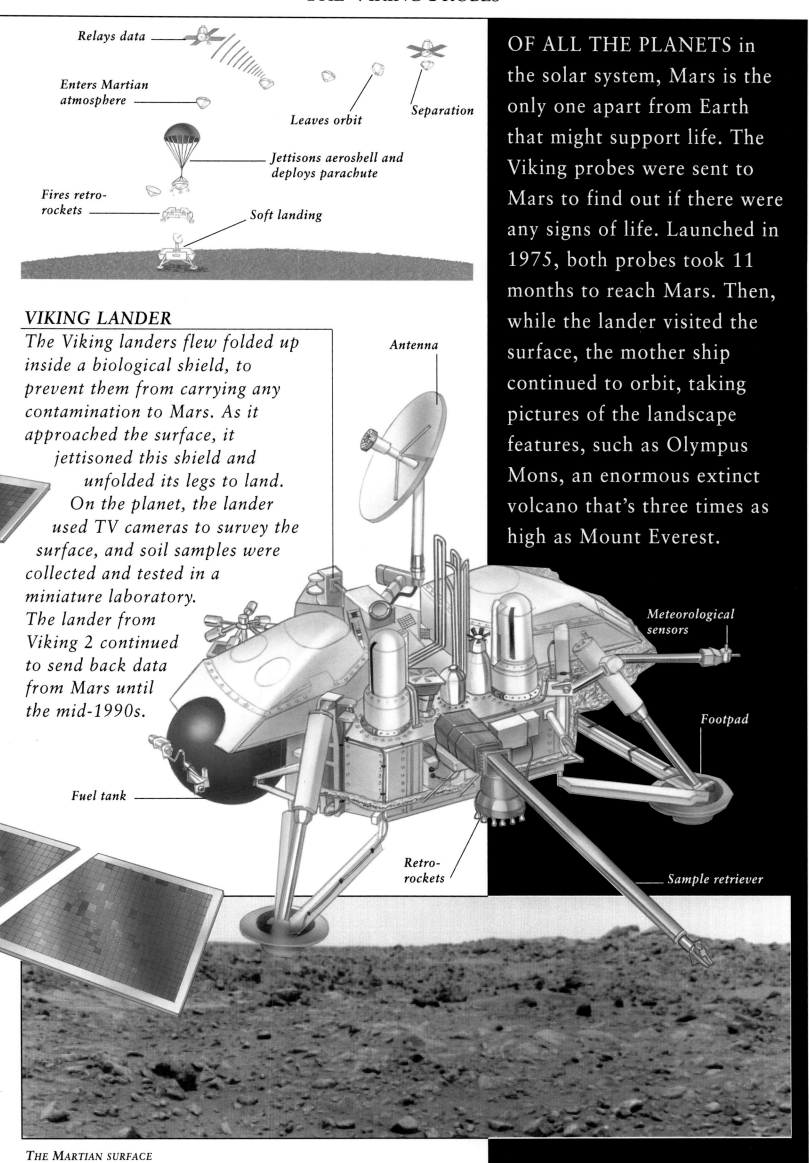

Relays data

Enters Martian atmosphere

Leaves orbit

Separation

Jettisons aeroshell and deploys parachute

Fires retro-rockets

Soft landing

VIKING LANDER

The Viking landers flew folded up inside a biological shield, to prevent them from carrying any contamination to Mars. As it approached the surface, it jettisoned this shield and unfolded its legs to land. On the planet, the lander used TV cameras to survey the surface, and soil samples were collected and tested in a miniature laboratory. The lander from Viking 2 continued to send back data from Mars until the mid-1990s.

Antenna

Meteorological sensors

Footpad

Fuel tank

Retro-rockets

Sample retriever

OF ALL THE PLANETS in the solar system, Mars is the only one apart from Earth that might support life. The Viking probes were sent to Mars to find out if there were any signs of life. Launched in 1975, both probes took 11 months to reach Mars. Then, while the lander visited the surface, the mother ship continued to orbit, taking pictures of the landscape features, such as Olympus Mons, an enormous extinct volcano that's three times as high as Mount Everest.

THE MARTIAN SURFACE

LIVING IN SPACE

LIFE ON BOARD
Space stations are not very comfortable. Cosmonauts tell of a loss of taste, and tend to eat spicy foods to compensate for this. Exercise is necessary to keep muscles strong, so an exercise bicycle and a treadmill have been installed.

COSMONAUTS hold the record for the length of time spent in space – first in the Salyut space station and then, since 1986, in Mir. Launched unmanned by a Proton rocket on February 20, 1986, Mir was first occupied in March that year, and has seldom been empty since. The station has improved crew accommodation, in comparison to its Salyut predecessors.

SALYUT
The Salyut series of space stations began with the launch of Salyut 1 on April 19, 1971. The first five Salyut stations had only one docking port, while Salyut's 6 and 7 had two. The addition of a second docking port allowed for the expansion of the station using the Cosmos module. During the fourteen years of Salyut missions, thousands of experiments were carried out.

SALYUT

Solar panel

Control consoles

Work and dining table

Aft docking port

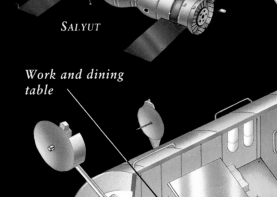

SKYLAB

SKYLAB
Skylab was made from the third-stage casing of the Saturn V rocket. It was damaged during launch and the astronauts had to rig up a parasol to stop it overheating. Skylab received three crews of astronauts during 1973 and reentered the atmosphere in 1979, scattering debris over the Indian Ocean and Australia.

MIR

Mir is 44 ft (13 m) long and 14 ft (4 m) in diameter. The main compartment takes up most of the spacecraft. It is attached at one end to a multi-docking module, and at the other to a propulsion compartment. There are two cabins, one on each side, where members of the crew eat, sleep, or make observations through portholes. Experiments are carried out inside the different modules attached to the main section.

Soyuz TM module

Docking ports

MIR WORK MODULE

DOCKING FACILITIES

The Mir space station is equipped with a special docking port that allows a range of other spacecraft to dock with it at the same time. Among these are the Kvant laboratory, Soyuz transfer craft, and Progress cargo craft. The intention was to use the facility to build up an entire space station.

SHUTTLE-MIR

In June 1995, the U.S. space shuttle Atlantis and Mir linked up in space. Atlantis chased Mir for two days, and they finally linked up 245 miles (392 km) above central Asia. The combined spacecraft held ten people for five days, including a replacement crew for Mir.

HANDSHAKE ON SHUTTLE-MIR LINK UP

SPACE STATION ALPHA

The space station Alpha will be an international scientific institute in space, supported by The United States, Europe, Canada, Japan, and the former Soviet Union. The design combines U.S. plans with those for a Mir follow-up station. The first element is due for launch in 1997. When finished, the station will weigh more than 400 tons, and consist of pressurized laboratories linked to living areas.

SPACE STATION ALPHA, WITH SHUTTLE

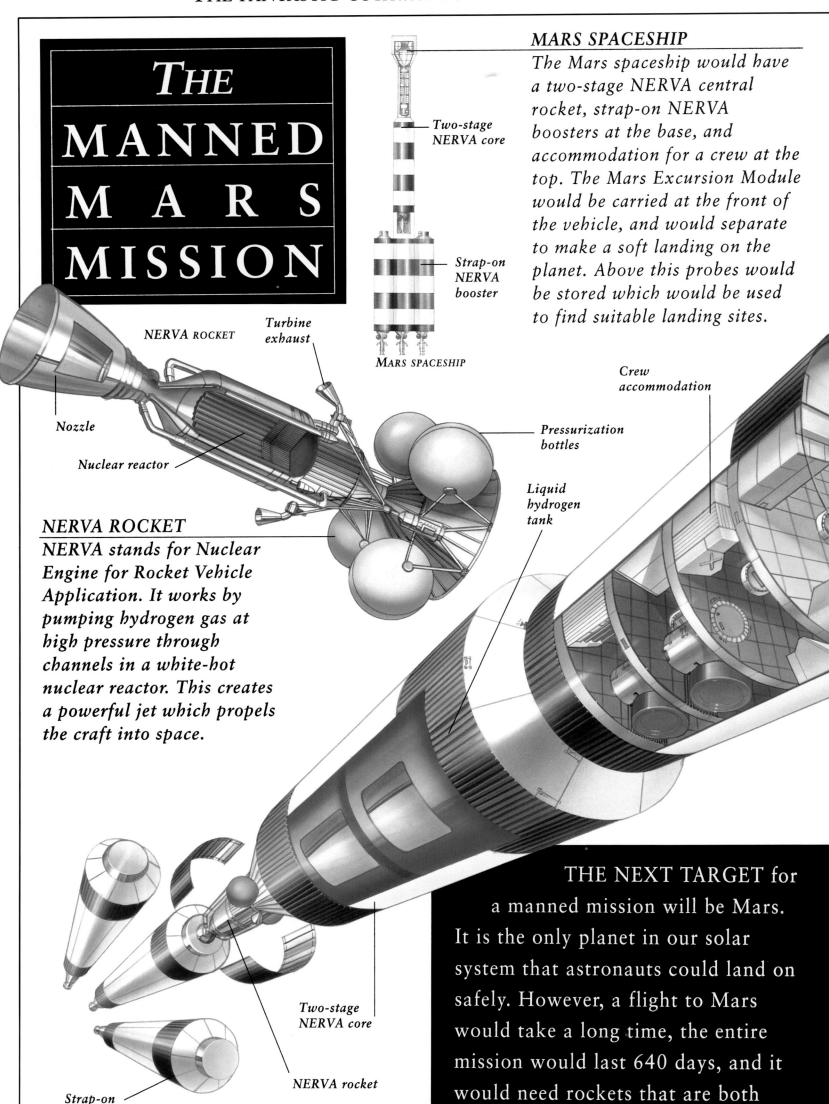

THE MANNED MARS MISSION

Two-stage NERVA core

Strap-on NERVA booster

MARS SPACESHIP

MARS SPACESHIP
The Mars spaceship would have a two-stage NERVA central rocket, strap-on NERVA boosters at the base, and accommodation for a crew at the top. The Mars Excursion Module would be carried at the front of the vehicle, and would separate to make a soft landing on the planet. Above this probes would be stored which would be used to find suitable landing sites.

NERVA ROCKET

Turbine exhaust

Nozzle

Nuclear reactor

Crew accommodation

Pressurization bottles

Liquid hydrogen tank

NERVA ROCKET
NERVA stands for Nuclear Engine for Rocket Vehicle Application. It works by pumping hydrogen gas at high pressure through channels in a white-hot nuclear reactor. This creates a powerful jet which propels the craft into space.

Two-stage NERVA core

NERVA rocket

Strap-on NERVA booster

THE NEXT TARGET for a manned mission will be Mars. It is the only planet in our solar system that astronauts could land on safely. However, a flight to Mars would take a long time, the entire mission would last 640 days, and it would need rockets that are both powerful and economical on fuel. The spacecraft would be out together

EXCURSION MODULE

The Mars Excursion Module consists of two separate stages mounted one on top of another. The upper, or ascent, stage will be used for escaping from Mars at the end of the mission. The descent stage would be left behind.

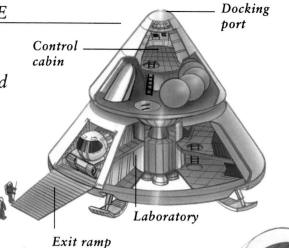

Docking port

Control cabin

Exit ramp

Laboratory

CREW ACCOMMODATION

The Mars spaceship would have enough accommodation for six astronauts. The Excursion Module would have room for a crew of three, while another three would remain in orbit around Mars.

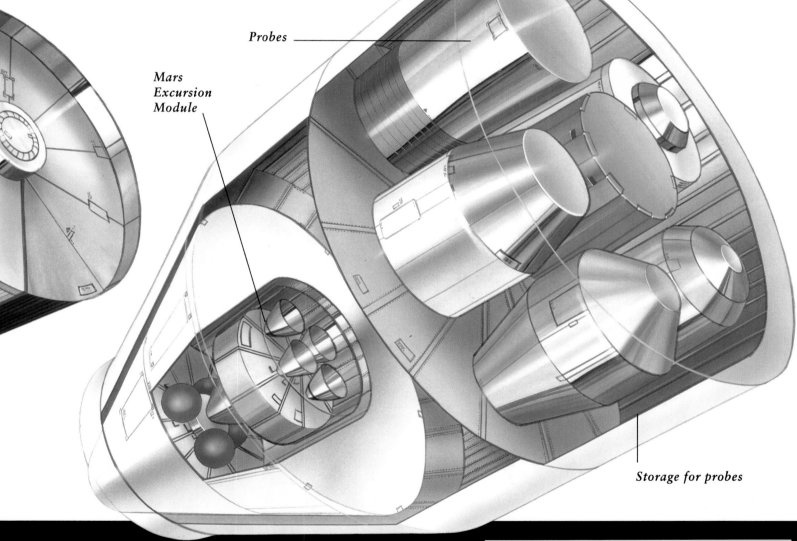

Probes

Mars Excursion Module

Storage for probes

in orbit around the Earth, with sections carried up a piece at a time. Once assembled in orbit, the rocket would only need a fraction of the thrust that the Saturn V used to reach the Moon. This is because the Earth's gravitational force is weaker here than on the ground. While on Mars the astronauts would explore the planet's surface for up to 30 days, before returning to orbit.

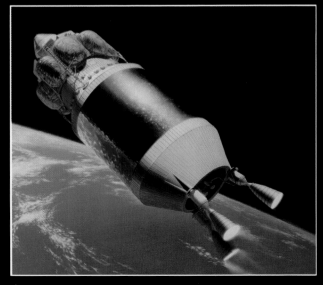

ASSEMBLING THE MISSION IN ORBIT

G L O S S A R Y

Altitude
Height above the Earth's surface.

Astronaut
A person who travels beyond the Earth's atmosphere and into space.

Booster
A rocket engine strapped to a spacecraft to give it extra thrust during the first seconds after launch.

Combustion chamber
The part of a rocket's engine where the fuel and oxidizer are mixed and then ignited (set fire to). This produces the exhaust gases which are channeled through a nozzle to create the thrust.

Cosmonaut
An astronaut of the Russian space program.

Escape velocity
The speed necessary to break free from the Earth's gravitational pull. This is 17,700 mph (28,500 km/h).

Gravity
The force of attraction between two large objects. The larger the object, the greater its gravitational force. The "pull" of the Earth's gravity must be overcome to launch a rocket into space.

Heat shield
The protective outer casing of a spacecraft which stops it from burning up when the craft reenters the Earth's atmosphere.

Launcher
A launch vehicle, or rocket engine, that carries a payload into space.

Module
A section of a spacecraft that can be separated from other sections.

NASA
The National Aeronautics and Space Administration, the United States' space agency based in Washington, D.C.

Nozzle
A cone-shaped attachment to a rocket which guides the exhaust gases down, giving the rockets the upward thrust it needs.

Orbit
The flight path of a spacecraft or satellite circling the Earth, Moon, or a planet. This can be either inclined (at an angle to the Equator), polar (over the North and South Poles), or geostationary (staying over the same spot).

Oxidizer
A substance containing oxygen that mixes with the fuel in a rocket engine, and enables the fuel to burn.

Payload
A rocket's cargo, such as a satellite.

Probe
An unmanned spacecraft.

Propellant
The substance burned in a rocket to produce thrust.

Satellite
An object orbiting a larger one. The Moon is a natural satellite of the Earth. There are now many man-made satellites orbiting the Earth.

Stage
One section of a rocket.

Thrust
The pushing force generated by a rocket's engine.

Thruster
Small rocket motor used to make minor adjustments to a spacecraft's position.

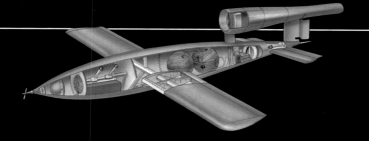

CHRONOLOGY

1903 Konstantin E. Tsiolkovsky publishes his scientific paper on the use of rockets for space travel.

1923 German scientist Hermann Oberth publishes a book on the technical problems of space flight.

1926 Robert Goddard launches the first liquid-propellant rocket.

1942 A German A-4 rocket reaches 60 miles (96 km).

1957 *October* The Soviet Union launches Sputnik 1, the first man-made satellite. *November* Launch of Sputnik 2, with dog Laika.

1958 *January* First U.S. satellite, Explorer 1, launched. *December* NASA launches first communications satellite.

1961 *April* Soviet cosmonaut Yuri Gagarin is the first man in space. *May* Alan Shepard is the first American in space.

1962 *February* John Glenn is the first American to orbit the Earth.

1963 *June* Cosmonaut Valentina Tereshkova is the first woman in space.

1964 *October* Three cosmonauts orbit the Earth in Voshkod 1.

1965 NASA's first manned Gemini flight. *July* U.S. probe Mariner 4 photographs Mars.

1967 *January* Three Apollo astronauts killed in launchpad fire. *June* Soviet probe Venera 4 transmits data on Venus' atmosphere.

1968 *October* First manned Apollo flight.

1969 *July* Apollo astronauts Neil Armstrong and Edwin "Buzz" Aldrin become the first men on the Moon.

1971 *May* Capsule from Soviet probe Mars 3 lands on Mars. *November* NASA's probe Mariner 9 is the first to orbit Mars.

1973 *May* Skylab 2 launched with a crew of three.

1975 *July* NASA's Apollo spacecraft docks with a Soyuz spacecraft. *October* Soviet probe Venera 9 lands on Venus and photographs the planet's surface.

1976 *July* NASA's Viking 1 sends photographs from Mars.

1977 *August, September* NASA launches Voyagers 1 and 2.

1981 *April* Launch of Columbia, NASA's first space shuttle, with astronauts John Young and Robert Crippen.

1983 *June* U.S. probe Pioneer 10 becomes the first spacecraft to travel beyond all the planets.

November Spacelab, built by the European Space Agency (ESA) is first launched in the space shuttle.

1986 *January* Space shuttle Challenger explodes shortly after launch, killing its crew of seven. *February* Launch of Soviet space station Mir. *March* ESA's probe Giotto passes Halley's comet and sends data and photographs.

1988 *September* U.S. manned space programs are resumed with launch of shuttle Discovery. *November* Unmanned Soviet space shuttle Buran launched by Energia rocket.

1990 Hubble Space Telescope launched.

1993 *December* Space shuttle mission to repair faulty mirror on the Hubble Space Telescope is successful.

1994 A variety of probes and satellites witness the collision between Jupiter and the Comet Shoemaker-Levy 9 which creates several enormous fireballs and punches holes in Jupiter's atmosphere.

1995 *June* Space Shuttle *Atlantis* docks successfully with Russian space station *Mir*. *July* Space probe *Galileo* launches mini-probe into Jupiter's atmosphere.

INDEX

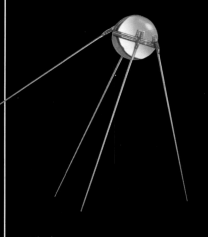

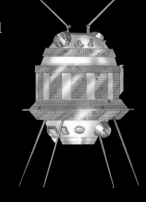

Photographic credits:

Abbreviations: t-top, m-middle, b-bottom, r-right, l-left

4, 5, 6t, 11: Hulton Deutsch Collection; 6m, 7b, 12, 13, 14, 15 all, 22, 23 both, 24l, 25 both, 27r, 28, 33, 34, 37: NASA; 6b: David Hardy; 7t: Novosti; 8, 10l, 16, 21r, 24r, 30, 31m, 35t: Frank Spooner Pictures; 9 both, 10r, 27l, 31t & b, 35b: Science Photo Library; 17, 19: European Space Agency; 18: Aerospatiale; 21l: Solution Pictures.

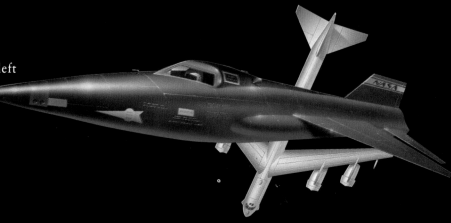